U.S. Department
of Transportation

**Research and
Special Programs
Administration**

Visitor Transportation Study:
Report on Urban Visitor Transportation Services

Prepared for:

U.S. Department of the Interior
National Park Service
National Capital Parks – Central

Washington, DC

Prepared by:

U.S. Department of Transportation
Research and Special Programs Administration
John A. Volpe National Transportation Systems Center

Cambridge, Massachusetts

February 2004

REPORT DOCUMENTATION PAGE

Public Reporting burden for this collection of information is estimated to average 1 hour per response, including the time for reviewing instructions, searching existing data sources, gathering and maintaining the data needed, and completing and reviewing the collection of information. Send comment regarding this burden estimates or any other aspect of this collection of information, including suggestions for reducing this burden, to Washington Headquarters Services, Directorate for information Operations and Reports, 1215 Jefferson Davis Highway, Suite 1204, Arlington, VA 22202-4302, and to the Office of Management and Budget, Paperwork Reduction Project (0704-0188,) Washington, DC 20503.

1. AGENCY USE ONLY (Leave Blank)	2. REPORT DATE February 2004	3. REPORT TYPE & DATES COVERED 2003-2004

4. TITLE AND SUBTITLE
Visitor Transportation Study: Report on urban visitor transportation services

5. FUNDING NUMBERS

6. AUTHORS
Sean Peirce, Jane Lappin

7. PERFORMING ORGANIZATION NAME(S) AND ADDRESS(ES)
U.S. Department of Transportation
Research and Special Programs Administration
John A. Volpe National Transportation Systems Center
55 Broadway
Cambridge, MA 02142

8. PERFORMING ORGANIZATION REPORT NUMBER

9. SPONSORING/MONITORING AGENCY NAME(S) AND ADDRESS(ES)
U.S. Department of the Interior
National Park Service
National Capital Parks – Central
900 Ohio Drive SW
Washington, DC 20024

10. SPONSORING AGENCY REPORT NUMBER

11. SUPPLEMENTARY NOTES

12a. DISTRIBUTION/AVAILABILITY

12b. DISTRIBUTION CODE

13. ABSTRACT
This report is part of a program of research designed to assist the National Park Service units of central Washington, DC, in their efforts to manage visitor mobility, reduce the negative environmental impacts of visitor transportation, and plan for the next generation of visitor transportation services. The approach taken is a review of successful practices in visitor transportation from five case-study cities: Boston, Savannah, Orlando, Philadelphia, and London. Each city offers lessons in two overlapping areas of interest: the design and operation of narrated visitor transportation services and broader policies and strategies for managing visitor transportation and mitigating its impacts.

14. KEY WORDS
national parks; Washington, DC; visitor transportation

15. NUMBER OF PAGES
46

16. PRICE CODE

SECURITY CLASSIFICATION OF REPORT None	*SECURITY CLASSIFICATION OF THIS PAGE* None	SECURITY CLASSIFICATION OF ABSTRACT None	LIMITATION OF ABSTRACT

TABLE OF CONTENTS

Executive Summary 1

I. Introduction 3

II. Methodology 5

III. Case Studies

Boston 6

Savannah 11

Orlando 16

Philadelphia 22

London 27

IV. Conclusions

General transportation management strategies 34

Specific recommendations for visitor transportation services 40

Summary 45

Appendix 46

Executive Summary

This report is part of a program of research designed to assist the National Park Service units of central Washington, DC, in their efforts to manage visitor mobility, reduce the negative environmental impacts of visitor transportation, and plan for the next generation of visitor transportation services. The approach taken is a review of successful practices in visitor transportation from five case-study cities: Boston, Savannah, Orlando, Philadelphia, and London. Each of these cities has its own unique set of visitor transportation issues, and none has a flawless approach. Nonetheless, each city offers lessons in two overlapping areas of interest to the NPS: the design and operation of narrated visitor transportation services, and more broadly, methods of managing visitor transportation and mitigating its impacts.

The report summarizes and synthesizes the findings from each of the five case studies. Broadly speaking, the principal points can be summarized as follows:

- In cities with historic downtowns, there is strong demand for both conventional public transit and for narrated sightseeing services. Sightseeing[*]services command a marked price premium, suggesting that there is a segment of visitors who derive significant value from their convenience and interpretation. Furthermore, there is a remarkable similarity across cities and companies in the pricing structures and service characteristics of the sightseeing services. Nearly all of the services studied feature 90- to 110-minute loops, with about 15 or 20 stops that serve top visitor destinations. Frequencies are usually in the range of every 20 to 30 minutes during peak times, with an all-day ticket costing in the range of $20 to $25. The strong similarity across cities implies that this combination of characteristics is well-suited to meet the needs of visitors and tour operators, and should be considered alongside the results from the Washington visitor surveys.

- The case studies also underscore the use of innovative design and convenience of service to increase use and market share of visitor transportation services. With respect to the vehicles themselves, the case studies all point to the value of using vehicles that are attractive and distinctive, yet appropriate to the context in which they operate. As the NPS considers a range of vehicles, this offers an opportunity to increase use through information technology and to reduce their environmental impacts through the use of alternative fuels. The case studies also highlight the rising public interest in more customizable itineraries, in novel experiences such as water travel, and in tours with special thematic links. Other priorities that emerge from the case studies are providing convenient connections to and from hotels and public transit stations, and using customer feedback to improve the service on an ongoing

---

* For the purposes of this report, "sightseeing" is an activity provided by private tour operators, or by public visitor transportation services operated by entities such as the NPS. This type of service generally includes educational components. The term "visitor transportation service" will generally be used when the discussion relates to the NPS.

basis.

- Independent of any changes to visitor transportation services, there are a number of steps that the NPS can take on its own to reduce the environmental impacts of visitor transportation in the Washington, DC area. Among these are improving the environments for walking and bicycling, providing public transit information in much greater detail on NPS websites and in orientation materials, and creating user fees associated with transportation impacts, such as parking fees or imposing peak-period surcharges in the vicinity of the National Mall.

- Every city struggles to balance visitor mobility with environmental stewardship and residents' quality of life. Reducing visitors' reliance on private vehicles and alleviating congestion can be brought about by a number of complementary strategies, including better regulation of traffic and tour buses, improved pedestrian-level wayfinding information, visitor-oriented public transit services or fare systems, the establishment of a gateway visitor center, and innovative marketing or partnership efforts such as a Visitor Card that bundles museum admission with visitor transportation and/or public transit passes.

- Each of these strategies is more effective when supported by a broad spectrum of stakeholders; indeed for some, extensive cooperation is indispensable. The NPS can be a key partner in working with other government agencies in the region, transit agencies, tourism promotion authorities, the travel and tourism industry, and other groups to develop mutually beneficial strategies for managing visitor transportation. This could be a formal effort such as Boston's Tourism Transportation Task Force or a set of ongoing collaborations. Either way, these groups can work together to promote congestion mitigation measures, improved visitor orientation and wayfinding materials, and additional public transportation options.

I. INTRODUCTION

The National Park Service units of central Washington, DC, serve a unique role. Among them are monuments to our nation's leaders and memorials of those who have died defending the country. They are places of national pride and solemn reflection. At the same time, they are located in the very center of one of the country's largest and most congested metropolitan areas, and receive millions of visitors each year. As such, they face significant challenges in managing visitor access and limiting the environmental impacts of transportation.

This report is part of a larger effort to analyze and assess visitor transportation needs in the National Mall and surrounding park areas. It uses a case-study approach to present information on best practices in visitor transportation planning, drawn from five other cities with large numbers of visitors and similar challenges. In particular, the report is designed to address three sets of interconnected challenges:
- to identify tools and strategies for the visitor transportation services in the National Mall and surrounding parking areas that will allow them to continue to meet visitor needs and NPS goals,
- to reduce traffic congestion in this dense urban area, and
- more broadly, to manage visitor transportation in a way that more effectively balances visitor mobility with environmental sustainability.

The case study method provides a measure of both breadth and depth. That is, a wide range of potential strategies are studied, but they are all drawn from a group of five cities so that sufficient background information can be presented about the context in which the strategies were developed and employed. The report also keeps in mind the National Park Service mission of resource conservation and visitor enjoyment. The case studies presented in the report thus address not only specific aspects of visitor transportation services, but also broader stewardship issues and public policies designed to mitigate the harmful effects of excess vehicle traffic, congestion, and pollution. In short, the report is designed to highlight examples of both *services* and *policies* that work to improve the accessibility of attractions, provide visitor mobility, minimize environmental impacts, promote visitor satisfaction, and enhance the interpretive quality of the visit.

In choosing the cities to serve as our case study examples, consideration was given to ensuring a broad spectrum of potential options and approaches. Consequently many of the services and strategies presented will not be directly transferable to Washington without some adaptation to local conditions. While we make note of potentially relevant differences between the case-study cities and Washington, detailed analysis of the extent to which a particular strategy would be suitable for Washington is beyond the scope of this report and has been reserved for a subsequent study.

The case study selection process began with a long list of US and foreign cities, which was augmented with suggestions from NPS staff. For these cities, basic data were collected on regional demographics, transit availability, visitor profiles and attractions, and forms of tourist transportation. Based on an evaluation of these factors, the five cities that showed the most promise for research were selected: Boston, Philadelphia, Savannah, Orlando, and London.

Section II of this report describes our research efforts and the structure of the case study reports. The case studies themselves make up Section III, and a review of conclusions and "lessons learned" from the case studies is presented in Section IV.

II. METHODOLOGY

Boston, Savannah, Orlando, Philadelphia, and London became the focus of the research efforts. For each city, we gathered background information on regional demographics and tourism trends from the Census, the local visitors' bureau, and other relevant sources. We researched the extent of traffic congestion problems, the availability of public transportation, and any efforts by the public sector to implement strategies for the management of tourist transportation. We gathered information on privately run transportation services and tours via internet searches and follow-up telephone interviews. (As stated in the Scope of Work, examples of visitor transportation from the National Park Service were generally not researched further, as these examples were assumed to be already known.) For each private transportation service, we gathered information on route options, vehicle types, fare structures, narration and interpretation, and specific transportation-related features such as accessibility to transit and outlying parking facilities.

Each of the case studies presented here thus consists of five parts:
- The context: background information on the city, its tourism market, and current transportation issues
- Public transportation: the type and extent of transit services available in the region, particularly those of use to visitors
- Tourist transportation management strategies: efforts by the public (and, where relevant, private) sector to enhance visitor mobility and/or mitigate the negative impacts of visitor transportation, including specific Alternative Transportation Systems (ATS)[1]
- Private transportation and tours: a description of the major tour services available in the city, with a particular focus on services similar to the NPS-contracted visitor transportation services in Washington, DC, and on any noteworthy or innovative features
- Implications for Washington: an overview of the potential for transferring aspects of the city's approach to Washington

---

[1] ATS is used throughout the report to refer to forms of transportation other than private motor vehicles.

III. CASE STUDIES

BOSTON

The context

Boston shares a number of similarities with Washington, DC. The two cities have roughly equal populations – 589,000 in Boston, 572,000 in Washington – surrounded by large metropolitan areas of roughly similar size (5.8 million for Boston, 7.6 million for Washington-Baltimore)[2]. The two regions also closely resemble each other with respect to traffic congestion. The Texas Transportation Institute's well-known Urban Mobility Study lists both cities as having Travel Time Indexes of 1.47, meaning essentially that road travel during peak periods takes 47 percent longer than it would under free-flowing traffic conditions. The cities are tied for 4th-worst in the country on this measure behind Los Angeles, San Francisco, and Chicago.

Boston and Washington are also magnets for tourism, particularly for visitors interested in American history. Boston itself is one of the nation's oldest cities and was one of the hubs of America's colonial and revolutionary periods. Popular tourist attractions from these periods include Faneuil Hall, Old North Church, and the Paul Revere House in central Boston, and Lexington and Concord where the first skirmishes of the revolution took place. Boston also has a long tradition as a center for literary and academic achievement, technological innovation, and social advocacy, and visitors are drawn to diverse sites such as Park Street Church, one of the spiritual homes of the abolitionist movement, Harvard University in Cambridge, Salem's House of the Seven Gables, and the Saugus Iron Works, one of America's first industrial complexes. All in all, the Boston region drew approximately 12.9 million visitors in 2002[3].

Public transportation

Public transportation in the Boston area is provided primarily by the Massachusetts Bay Transportation Authority (MBTA). MBTA service is quite extensive and includes 4 subway lines, 162 bus routes, 12 commuter rail lines, and 4 ferry lines. As in Washington, visitors to Boston tend to make frequent use of the subway system in particular; its four lines converge in downtown Boston and together provide service to almost all of the city's major visitor destinations, including historic sites, museums, hotels, restaurants, and the airport. Suburban destinations beyond the reach of the subway lines can generally be reached by either bus (Lexington) or commuter rail (Salem, Concord). To give a sense of the extent to which visitors can rely on transit to access destinations, the following chart lists the distances from some major attractions to the nearest MBTA service.[4] As the chart shows, many of the top destinations are within a quarter-mile of transit service, and most are within a half-mile.

---

[2] Census.
[3] Greater Boston C&VB.
[4] Source: MBTA online trip planner and site visits. Excludes some low-frequency bus routes where subway service is available nearby.

Destination	Nearest service(s)	Distance	Approximate walking time
Faneuil Hall	State Street subway station Government Center subway station	0.15 miles 0.25 miles	3 minutes 5 minutes
Old South Meeting House	State Street subway station	Adjacent	0 minutes
Old North Church	Haymarket subway station	0.31 miles	6 minutes
Paul Revere House	Haymarket subway station Aquarium subway station	0.36 miles 0.39 miles	7 minutes 8 minutes
U.S.S. Constitution	Route 93 bus stop	0.08 miles	2 minutes
New England Aquarium	Long Wharf dock for harbor ferries Aquarium subway station	0.11 miles 0.11 miles	2 minutes 2 minutes
Harvard University	Harvard Square subway station	Adjacent	0 minutes
Museum of Fine Arts	Museum streetcar station Ruggles subway station	0.05 miles 0.36 miles	1 minute 7 minutes
John F. Kennedy NHS	Route 66 bus stop Coolidge Corner streetcar stop	0.12 miles 0.41 miles	2 minutes 8 minutes
Lexington Battle Green	Route 76 bus stop	Adjacent	0 minutes
Salem Maritime NHS	Routes 451/465 bus stop Salem commuter rail station	0.12 miles 0.43 miles	2 minutes 9 minutes
Adams NHS visitor center	Quincy Center subway station	0.30 miles	6 minutes

The MBTA offers tourist-oriented 1-, 3-, and 7-day passes, which allow unlimited use of the subways, buses, and inner harbor ferries as well as the innermost sections of the commuter rail network. These passes are available for sale via the MBTA website and at numerous subway stations and hotels in the area.

Tourist transportation management strategies

Boston's principal strategy for visitor transportation is to promote walking and public transit, both for the environmental benefits and as a way of allowing visitors to get a first-hand sense of the city's neighborhoods. Boston bills itself as "America's Walking City" and its promotional materials stress the ease with which visitors can travel around the city on foot and by transit. This philosophy takes physical expression in the form of the Freedom Trail, a 2½-mile red line in the sidewalk connecting sixteen historic sites (many of which are part of Boston National Historical Park) in downtown Boston and Charlestown.

Most travel guidebooks agree with the assessment that Boston is best experienced on foot, suggesting that visitors forego the difficulty of driving and parking in the city and rely instead on walking, MBTA service, and taxis. Visitors to Boston who are arriving by car but nonetheless prefer not to drive into the city center can avail themselves of one the MBTA's park-and-ride lots, connecting to the subway system at outlying stations such as Alewife, Riverside, and Braintree that are near highway interchanges. These park-and-ride locations are noted on highway signage approaching the city, on MBTA maps, and in trip-planning materials provided by the Massachusetts Office of Travel and Tourism and other tourism agencies.

Concern about the problems caused by tour buses led the City of Boston in 2001 to convene a multi-stakeholder task force to address these issues, particularly the pollution and congestion caused by tour buses. This Task Force included representatives from the city, the NPS, the travel and tourism industry, private tour operators, historical associations, and neighborhood groups. Many months of discussion and study led to a series of recommendations, which the city has now largely implemented[5]. Notably, the Boston Transportation Department (BTD) has set aside 12 curbside areas throughout the city center as drop-off/pick-up zones for tour buses. These zones are for the exclusive use of tour buses, with each bus limited to 15 minutes. For longer-term parking, bus layover facilities were created at two satellite locations, both of which are just outside of downtown. The BTD has begun distributing a detailed map of these curbside and layover facilities to tour operators to help them navigate through the downtown.

In exchange for accommodating tour buses in this way, the city has stepped up its enforcement of parking rules. Tour buses are not permitted to use commercial loading zones, metered parking spaces, or MBTA bus stops, and are prohibited from idling for more than 5 minutes. BTD has created a one-page summary sheet of these regulations for distribution to tour bus operators along with the map of designated parking areas.

Boston has a number of small visitor centers and orientation points rather than one major center. These include the National Park Service visitor center and Boston Harbor Islands visitor booth, visitor information centers on Boston Common and at the Prudential Center, and the Cambridge information booth in Harvard Square. All of these sites are within about one-tenth of a mile of MBTA subway stations (in some cases, directly across the street from station entrances). They are also all either adjacent to or within a few blocks of private parking facilities. However, none has the capacity to receive tour buses or serve as a transportation hub.

Private transportation and tours
Private tour options in Boston include hop-on/hop-off circulating trolleys, river and harbor tours, the amphibious Duck Tours, and walking tours.

Trolley tours: Several different companies – Discover Boston, Gray Line, and Historic Tours of America – offer competing trolley tours, but the main outlines of the services

---

[5] http://www.cityofboson.gov/transportation/tour_bus.asp

are quite similar. All three are narrated tours running between 90 and 110 minutes in length, using antique-style trolley buses, making 17 or 18 stops in central Boston. Trolleys depart as often as every 15-20 minutes during peak times and roughly every 25-30 at other times. The tours are also quite similar with respect to price, with a one-day pass (including unlimited re-boarding privileges) selling for $24 or $25. Each of the tours also has some distinct features and services of note:

- Discover Boston Trolley Tours provides "Audiomate" devices (telephone-like handsets, similar to those seen in museums) to non-English speaking travelers, allowing them to receive the tour's commentary in Spanish, French, German, Italian, or Japanese.
- Gray Line (Beantown Trolley) offers connecting bus transportation to and from suburban hotels to the trolley tour starting point.
- Historic Tours of America include either a 45-minute cruise on Boston Harbor (in season) or a multimedia presentation on the battle of Bunker Hill.

River and harbor tours: There are also several waterborne tours of the city, operating either along the Charles River or in Boston Harbor. The Charles Riverboat Company offers 75- and 90-minute tours of Boston and Cambridge, running up and down the Charles River in Victorian-styled riverboats and paddleboats ($10). These river tours depart from a dock at the Cambridgeside Galleria shopping mall, which is connected by a free shuttle bus to the Kendall Square subway station and is within walking distance (one-third of a mile) of Lechmere station. Parking is also available in the mall's onsite parking garage ($1 for the first hour, $20 per day).

Boston Harbor Cruises runs a number of services in the harbor, including a 45-minute sightseeing cruise, a 45-minute cruise to Charlestown to see the U.S.S. Constitution, and a 90-minute sunset cruise. The company also operates ferry services to the Boston Harbor Islands National Recreation Area under contract with the NPS. All services cost $12 and depart from Long Wharf in downtown Boston. Long Wharf is next to the Aquarium subway station and the Harbor Garage parking facility. It is also home to the Boston Harbor Islands visitor booth and is a stop for all three of the sightseeing trolleys described above. As such, Long Wharf acts as a multimodal transportation node and a locus for information, highlighting the value of promoting informal coordination between private- and public-sector service providers. Reducing tourists' guesswork by providing easy connections between services (public transit, private sightseeing, ferries) and onsite orientation can only promote visitor satisfaction and help with the perception that ATS is convenient to use.

Amphibious tours: Duck Tours are Boston's version of the land-and-water tours that have been developed in cities around the country using World War II-era amphibious vehicles. Visitors can join the Duck Tour at either the Prudential Center or the Museum of Science, both of which offer on-site transit connections and commercial parking. The tour itself is an 80-minute narrated tour of the city, covering Charlestown, the North End, downtown, and the Back Bay, plus a splash into the Charles River. Tickets are $23.

As with the trolley tours and sightseeing boats, the Duck Tours are private, for-profit operations whose costs are covered by the company's capital structure and operating revenues. It is also important to keep in mind that these tours all aim to entertain as much as to inform, and their narration is therefore inherently more "commercial" and less edifying than it would be if it were offered by a strictly educational group or by the NPS itself.

Walking tours: Boston by Foot is a non-profit organization that offers walking tours of the city, focused on architecture and history. The tours are led by volunteer guides and are offered daily from May through October. Seven different 90-minute tours are available, most of which are 90 minutes in length and are focused on a particular historic neighborhood; there is also a 60-minute tour that is specifically designed for children. Tours are $9 ($6 for the shorter children's tour).

Implications for Washington

The Boston case study highlights the roles of *walking, public transit, and intermodal connections*. Walking is in many ways the ideal form of urban visitor transportation since it costs nothing, creates no pollution, and allows visitors to move at their own pace and gain a much more intimate view of the city than they would from a moving vehicle. Of course, walking is more useful in places such as Boston where visitor attractions are clustered within a small geographic area; many of the stops along the Freedom Trail, for example, are not more than a quarter-mile apart.

For longer distances, transit is complementary to walking, uses existing infrastructure and services, and is environmentally friendly. It is particularly convenient when stations are within an easy walking distance of visitor destinations. Promoting transit use in these cases then becomes largely a question of improved information – making an unfamiliar transit system as easy and convenient to use as possible. Some specific strategies that emerge from the Boston case study include:

- Creating a 3- or 4-day discounted visitor transit pass, to better align with the average length of stay in DC, which is 3.1 nights[6];
- Allowing visitor transit passes to be used on both rail and bus services, rather than just one or the other. This would help visitors reach sites that are beyond easy walking distance of Metrorail stations.
- Improving street-level wayfinding materials to make walking routes clear. While a stripe on the sidewalk may not be as practical in Washington, additional directional signs, maps, and directional "blazes" would be useful.

Another lesson from Boston is the value of *coordination with stakeholders in the public and private sectors*. This includes small details such as ensuring that trolley tours make stops that allow passengers to connect to other modes of transport (such as sightseeing boats and public transit), and larger endeavors such as participating in multi-stakeholder task forces to develop comprehensive plans for managing tourist transportation.

---

[6] Washington, DC Convention and Tourism Corporation, *2002 Visitor Statistics Press Briefing*.

Stakeholder coordination is particularly important because of the way the National Mall and surrounding parks are interwoven with its urban environment – efforts by the NPS to reduce congestion and pollution will be compromised if they are not matched by compatible policies from the District of Columbia and cooperation from the private sector.

With respect to the current sightseeing services, it is clear from the Boston case study that circulating, hop-on/hop-off trolleys are popular with the public and provide value to visitors at a price point of around $24. Some potential innovations that are suggested include *providing more multilingual interpretation* for overseas visitors and *providing connecting bus service from suburban hotels* to the trolley departure point, so that visitors staying outside the city can access the tour without having to drive into the city. It is also clear from looking at the range of services available that a variety of travel modes, vehicle types, and tour approaches can be successful. *Water-based transportation* in particular seems to be popular, providing a unique perspective on the city and a valued visitor experience. This suggests the possibility of a boat tour that might, for example, allow visitors to view the major memorials from the Potomac River.

Boston: Summary of effective practices
General strategies:
Promote walking and public transit, for example with pedestrian-level wayfinding signage
Create a 3- or 4-day visitor-oriented transit pass valid on both trains and buses
Establish a formal procedure for coordinating with stakeholders on visitor transportation management
For sightseeing or visitor transportation services:
Provide multilingual interpretation options
Consider adding connecting bus service to hotels
Study possibility of water-based transportation

SAVANNAH

The context
Savannah is a city of 132,000 people (with a metropolitan area of 293,000 people),[7] situated along Georgia's Atlantic coastline. Founded in 1733, Savannah was Georgia's first city and served for many years as the colonial capital. The city was laid out by James Oglethorpe in a distinctive grid pattern, punctuated by attractive squares, that remains largely intact. Savannah avoided destruction during the Civil War when General Sherman, struck by its beauty, presented the city to President Lincoln as a Christmas gift in 1864. Savannah's beauty continues to attract visitors. In 2000, the city had about 2.2

---

[7] Census 2000.

million overnight visitors, many of whom are drawn by its historic streets and buildings, the waterfront, and nearby plantations. Savannah is also a destination for those interested in the Gullah culture of the coastal low country, and is well-known for its Saint Patrick's Day parade.

Public transportation

Public transportation in Savannah is provided by Chatham Area Transit (CAT). CAT runs 20 different bus routes throughout the city and Chatham County; fares are $1. CAT also runs a special bus route of particular interest to visitors: the Historic Area Shuttle, also called the Downtown Loop. This bus service consists of a 30-stop loop through Savannah's historic district, starting and ending at the visitor's center and stopping at or near most of the historic squares, buildings, museums, and hotels in the historic district[8]. Five of the shuttle stops are connection points to other scheduled CAT bus services and to the Savannah Belles Ferry, a river service that links the downtown to the convention center. The Historic Area Shuttle uses buses that resemble old-fashioned trolley cars but are in fact fully accessible to visitors with disabilities. No narration is provided. Unlike other CAT services, the Historic Area Shuttle is free of charge, with the city of Savannah contributing 50 percent of its operating costs[9] as a way of promoting tourism and mitigating congestion. This funding comes from a per-passenger charge that the city levies on private tour companies who operate in the downtown area.

The Historic Area Shuttle service runs seven days a week, with buses arriving every 20 minutes during peak times and seasons, and every 40 minutes during off-peak times. While originally designed primarily for visitors, it has also become popular with local residents as it provides service to a supermarket, health center, and other services. Surveys showed that the shuttle's ridership is nearly evenly split between residents and visitors, with total ridership in 2002 nearing 200,000.

Tourist transportation management strategies

Savannah has had to manage transportation demand very carefully because of the large number of people who visit its 2½ square-mile historic district. This has been particularly true in the past decade, with a surge in tourism since the publication of *Midnight in the Garden of Good and Evil*. One of the principal elements of the city's strategy is an ordinance which requires the licensure of tour operators and tightly regulates tour vehicles' use of city streets and curbside space. Tour operators are required to submit detailed routing plans for approval by the City. Once operational, they may use only designated areas for layover parking and passenger loading/unloading, must use designated routes, and may not make more than one trip around a particular square

---

[8] See http://www.catchacat.org/catchacat/shuttle.htm for timetables and other information.

[9] The remaining costs are covered by CAT's budget. It is important to keep in mind that most CAT bus routes (and indeed most transit services in the US) cover less than 50 percent of their costs through farebox revenue.

during the same tour[10]. (The Historic Area Shuttle and other public transit services are exempt from these regulations.)

Another part of Savannah's strategy for managing visitor flows is to drive home the message to visitors that they will enjoy their visit much more if they stop at the Savannah Visitor Information Center and transfer to some form of ATS – be it walking, the Historic Area Shuttle, or a sightseeing service – rather than attempt to drive straight into the historic district. This message is conveyed through the marketing materials and visitor guides developed by the Savannah Chamber of Commerce and Savannah Area Convention and Visitors Bureau. For example, the Getting to Savannah page of the Savannah media guide describes the visitor center as "your first stop" and all of the driving directions provided lead directly (and only) there. The text of the guide also subtly mentions the virtues leaving one's car parked, mentioning in the introduction that:

> "[Savannah's] streets are waiting to be discovered at your own leisurely pace by foot, by trolley, by sea or by majestic steed and coachman tour guide whose carriage awaits to fulfill your inquisitiveness… To sample the true charisma of Savannah, visitors must walk the city streets and visit our charming squares. Massive oaks, with branches veiled in Spanish moss, announce you are in the true Old South."[11]

As in Boston, the idea is reinforced that walking and other alternative forms of transportation are not only convenient, but in fact the ideal way to see and experience the city in all of its unique aspects. These marketing materials shape visitors' expectations by describing walking as *the* way to see the city. The potentially slower rate of travel is turned into an essential attribute of the visitor experience – a leisurely pace that allows one to savor fine details and truly gain an appreciation of the city. Likewise, visitors are encouraged to seek orientation at the visitor center in order to gain a deeper appreciation of the stories that the city has to tell, rather than drive through on their own.

As a practical matter, highway signage along the routes into the city also alerts drivers to the presence of the visitor center. Staff from the Savannah center also coordinate with the state-run Georgia Welcome Center (on Interstate 95 near the South Carolina border) to ensure that the orientation staff there also encourage visitors to make the Savannah visitor center their first stop.

The center itself is strategically located – on one of the main routes into the city, within reasonable walking distance of the historic district but with ample on-site parking (over 300 car spaces, plus spaces for tour buses). It therefore serves as something of a transportation hub. Car travelers coming into town on US 17 or I-16 can stop at the visitor center on their way into town, park their car, and pick up orientation materials or speak with a representative. From there, they can then walk (about 10 minutes) or take the CAT shuttle into the historic district. The same goes for tour bus travelers when their buses use the center as a layover area.

---

[10] Volpe Center, Tour Bus Management Initiative Best Practices Report.
[11] Savannah Area Convention and Visitors Bureau.
http://www.savcvb.com/pressroom/CVBmediaguide.pdf

Moreover, the visitor center is a major hub for private tours, with the city leasing "slots" in the parking area to private tour services. The popularity of the visitor center, and the city's success in steering visitors to it, is measured by the fact that most (though not all) of Savannah's tours, whether by bus, trolley, horse-drawn carriage, or on foot, use the visitor center lot as a point of departure. This has allowed Savannah to moderate traffic congestion and parking demand in the historic district[12].

Private transportation and tours

As in Boston, there are several different competing trolley tours in Savannah, but most of them share similar characteristics. Gray Line, Historic Tours of America, and Savannah Tours all offer circulating trolley tours of the Savannah historic district using similar antique-style trolley buses. Each company has at least some vehicles that are accessible to the handicapped. All three tours cover largely the same territory, and the pricing structures and business models are also very similar. Specifically, each of the tour companies offers three tiers of service:

- A 90-minute, fully narrated tour of the historic district (adult price: $19 Gray Line; $20 Historic Tours; $18 Old Savannah)
- The same tour, but with the addition of on-and-off privileges all day at any of 13 or 14 stops, with trolleys passing roughly every 20 minutes during peak times and seasons ($21 Gray Line; $24 Historic Tours; $21 Old Savannah)
- The circulating trolley tour with on-and-off privileges, plus a pass for admission to one or more historic homes or museums ($24 Gray Line; $26 Historic Tours; $25-27 Old Savannah)

As mentioned above, these tours all use the visitor center as one of their starting and stopping points, although they also offer the option of starting the tour at their own welcome center or indeed at any of the stops along the route. Tickets are sold on board and reservations are not required. Each of the companies also arranges for connecting shuttle transportation from area hotels; as mentioned earlier, this reduces the need for visitors to drive around the city during their stay.

In addition to these conventional tours, each of the companies offers additional options, such as a river cruise or evening ghost tour. Of particular interest is the Savannah Experience Tour offered by Old Savannah, which ventures outside of the historic district to bring visitors to some of Savannah's most interesting – but less-visited – neighborhoods and historic sites. This narrated mini-bus tour departs twice a day and costs $25.

Other tour options include carriage tours, walking tours, and bicycle tours:
- Historic Savannah Carriage Tours offers 50- to 60-minute narrated tours of the major sights in the historic district using horse-drawn carriages; tours depart roughly hourly

---

[12] Volpe Center, Tour Bus Management Initiative Best Practices Report.

from Madison Square and from the Hyatt Regency hotel. A special ghost-oriented tour is available at twilight hours.

- "Ghost Talk Ghost Walk" is a 90-minute walking tour of the historic district that focuses on ghosts, largely inspired by Margaret DeBolt's *Savannah Specters*. The tour runs once a day, starting around dusk, and costs $10.
- Discover Adventures operates a multi-day tour of the Savannah area that includes walking tours of the historic district and bicycle excursions to nearby towns and beaches. Historic sights are included in the itinerary alongside outdoor recreation such as sea kayaking. This is a much more comprehensive package that includes lodging and is therefore not in the same genre as other visitor transportation services, but it is included here to give a sense of the range of visitor options on the market.

Implications for Washington

Savannah is often cited as an example of a city where several complementary strategies come together to reduce private vehicle use and tourism-related congestion. These include:

- Carefully regulating tourist-oriented transportation offerings,
- Setting (and enforcing) restrictions on the operation and routing of tour vehicles within the historic district,
- Ensuring that sources of travel information, such as marketing brochures and on-site orientation materials, stress the value of experiencing the city on foot or via other forms of ATS, and
- Establishing a "gateway"-type visitor center that serves triple duty: i.e., as a point of orientation, as a departure point for tour services, and as a site for remote parking for visitors transferring from cars and buses onto smaller ATS vehicles or to pedestrian travel.

Implementing these strategies in Washington would of course require extensive cooperation with partners in the public and private sectors, especially if additional regulation is to be considered. In addition, it is worth noting that the particular circumstances that make the Savannah Visitor Information Center successful as a transportation hub – proximity to the historic district and main highways, availability of ample parking – are unlikely to be found in the same combination anywhere in the District of Columbia. Significant additional study of feasibility would therefore be necessary before a strategy employing a gateway visitor center could be seriously considered.

What is perhaps more directly transferable is the broader theme of providing ATS information to visitors in multiple forms, both pre-trip and en route. As the Savannah brochure suggests, *marketing materials* can stress – in a creative, friendly way – the benefits of ATS and discourage private vehicle travel. *Highway signage* should also direct visitors to remote parking wherever it is available. Again, this strategy requires coordination with Chambers of Commerce and other private tourism-promotion groups as well as with the public sector.

In terms of designing specific visitor transportation services, Savannah's *free downtown shuttle* provides an example of a transportation service that provides mobility for visitors and residents alike, and which makes it easy for visitors to leave their cars in remote parking lots. Even with a free shuttle, however, the privately run hop-on/hop-off trolleys are still a popular option. The various competing services have largely the same service characteristics: a 90-minute loop with trolleys departing every 20 minutes during peak periods, and with tickets costing $21 to $24. Some of the specific keys to the success of these trolleys include *easy connections to the visitor center and remote parking*, and *free connecting transportation* from local hotels to the trolley route.

Savannah's array of tour services also suggests that *there is interest in a very wide range of tour services and transportation modes*. Trolley services that circulate among the typical tourist sights are still quite popular, but visitors are also showing strong interest in twilight and evening tours, riverboats, walking tours, carriage tours, and excursions to other points of interest beyond the historic district. There is also, perhaps in keeping with national trends toward more active recreation, distinctive trips, and "adventure" travel, an interest in tours that combine walking, cycling, and outdoor recreation. While the NPS is unlikely to get into the business of providing every conceivable tour variant and excursion package, it is worth noting the public's growing interest in a diversity of tour options. Additional evening tours could be considered along with the possibility of Potomac River services, or tour packages that bring visitors to destinations outside the typical circuit.

Savannah: Summary of effective practices
General strategies:
Establish a gateway visitor center to provide orientation and facilitate transfers from cars and tour buses to ATS
Use marketing materials to highlight the special virtues of exploring the city on foot
Provide a free or low-cost downtown shuttle
For sightseeing or visitor transportation services:
Provide convenient connections to the visitor center and parking
Consider travelers' interests in diverse tour options and modes of travel

ORLANDO

The context

The Orlando metropolitan area is home to some of America's best-known tourist destinations. Though the city of Orlando has only 186,000 residents, the metro area is home to 1.6 million people as well as attractions such as Disney's Magic Kingdom theme park and Epcot Center, Universal Studios, and Sea World, a marine amusement park. Orlando is the 4th-most popular US destination for overseas visitors behind New York,

Los Angeles, and Miami, having hosted over 1.8 million overseas visitors in 2002[13]. All in all, the area drew over 40 million visitors in 2000, over three-quarters of whom were leisure travelers[14].

Orlando's traffic congestion problem is not as severe as in other cities. The most recent data show that Orlando's roads have a travel time index of 1.32, making it the 23rd-worst region in the country[15]. However, Orlando's congestion index has been consistently on the rise since the early 1980s, meaning that it is an increasingly important concern.

Public transportation

Many of the Orlando area's attractions are spread out in a corridor to the southwest of the city, with Disney World nearly 20 miles from downtown. Most guidebooks to Orlando accordingly recommend that visitors rent a car, as it is not really practical to get around solely by public transportation; this is likely especially true for the 43 percent of leisure visitors who are there with their families[16]. All of this is not to say, however, that public transportation is not available in the Orlando area or that it is not useful for certain trips.

Of particular interest is the "Lymmo" service run by the Central Florida Regional Transportation Authority, better known as Lynx. The Lynx Lymmo is a free shuttle service that runs in a 19-stop loop through the innermost sections of downtown Orlando. It was originally planned as a joint venture between Lynx and the City of Orlando as a way to reduce parking demand in the downtown area. The City of Orlando continues to make financial contributions in order to keep the Lymmo service free of charge.

Lymmo service has proven popular and successful, and has been upgraded to a Bus Rapid Transit service with a dedicated traffic lane and signal priority. The buses themselves are low-floor, accessible models than run on compressed natural gas, with a frequency of every 5 minutes during peak periods and every 10 minutes at other times.

The Lymmo provides service to downtown office buildings, city hall, the courthouse, and the Orlando arena, but is many miles from the major theme parks and serves very few tourist-oriented destinations. As such, Lynx managers characterized its ridership as consisting mostly of downtown workers, with relatively few tourists except during special events. Still, the success of a downtown shuttle bus in a region as sprawling and car-dependent as Orlando suggests that travelers are willing to choose "alternative" transportation when it is made fast, convenient, and inexpensive. Focus groups with Lymmo riders highlight the fact that people perceive the Lymmo as distinct from other Lynx transit service, with comments such as "Lymmo is different. It is just downtown" and "It is not like riding the regular bus."[17] Part of Lymmo's perceived distinctiveness

---

[13] US Commerce Department, Office of Travel & Tourism Industries. "Overseas visitors to select US cities/Hawaiian islands 2002-2001." For these purposes, "overseas" excludes Canada and Mexico.
[14] Orlando/Orange County CVB.
[15] Texas Transportation Institute, Urban Mobility Study.
[16] Orlando/Orange County CVB.
[17] Central Florida Regional Transportation Authority, *2001 Lynx Market Research Study*.

may also stem from its physical appearance: the buses are painted in eye-catching color schemes as part of a public-art program, and the stations themselves are also brightly colored.

Tourist transportation management strategies

The I-Ride Trolley is a bus transportation service that runs on two routes in the International Drive area, a major convention/resort area about 15 miles southwest of downtown Orlando. The two routes cover 78 stops and provide service to hotels, restaurants, retail shops, the Orange County Convention Center, and tourist attractions such as Sea World, Dolly Parton's Dixie Stampede, and numerous water parks and mini-golf courses. The service is operated with accessible, antique-type trolley buses, with vehicles arriving every 20 minutes on the main route and every 30 minutes on the secondary route. One-way trips cost 75 cents, which includes a free transfer to the other trolley route if needed. A range of discounted passes is also available.

I-Ride is the result of a public-private partnership between local businesses and the city and county governments. It is funded by a special, voluntary property-tax assessment on businesses in the area, levied under the auspices of three Municipal Service Taxing Units. The partnership was established to promote tourism and reduce traffic congestion in the area. It sees I-Ride as a way to do both, since allowing tourists and conventioneers to access a wide range of visitor attractions without having to get in their cars or fight traffic is both a congestion mitigation measure and a distinct marketing advantage. I-Ride carries about 1.7 million passengers a year, the vast majority of whom are visitors who prefer not to drive. However, some of the ridership is also drawn from Orlando-area residents, particularly those who are employees of area businesses.

Consistent with other visitor-orientation systems, I-Ride has found that distinctive vehicles are a key component to making the system work. I-Ride's ridership levels rose dramatically when conventional transit-style buses were replaced with the colorful vintage trolley buses.

The Orlando area has also developed advanced traveler information systems (ATIS) for those who choose to drive. A partnership between the Florida Department of Transportation and the University of Central Florida resulted in the creation of a dedicated 511 telephone line[18] for information on Interstate 4, the main highway in the region. The system uses interactive voice recognition software to provide updated, area-specific information on congestion and travel delays. (There is also an accompanying website, http://www.trafficinfo.org, that provides information in greater detail.) The goal of these systems is to allow travelers to make better-informed travel decisions – and thus to avoid congestion whenever possible, or at least make allowances for it in their schedules.

---

[18] In 2000, the Federal Communications Commission designated 511 as the nationwide three-digit number for traveler information, much like 411 for directory assistance. Decisions about information options and implementation were left up to individual states and localities.

Whether or not traffic congestion can be alleviated solely through better information provision is a question of some debate, though at present the Orlando 511 system is neither comprehensive enough nor well-used enough to make much of a dent in regional congestion levels. The ability to learn about and plan for travel delays is nonetheless a definite benefit for individual travelers. Other states and regions of the country have also launched 511 systems; a number of these cover public transit as well as traffic, and some even have information on local National Parks[19].

Private transportation and tours

As far as we could determine, there are no circulating hop-on/hop-off tours of the Orlando area, which is not surprising given the region's spatial layout and types of attractions. Most of the private tour services that are offered are half-day and daylong excursions to other areas in Florida, such as Cape Canaveral.

One privately run transportation system that is of particular interest is that of Disney World. This is in part because of the sheer scale of its operations. The Disney World complex hosted 14 million visitors[20] in 2002, only slightly less than the entire Washington metropolitan area; it includes within its boundaries four theme parks, two water parks, 18 themed resort hotels, and numerous restaurants, retail shops, entertainment venues, and other amenities. Moving visitors amongst these sites is a vast undertaking, with Disney's transportation division employing about 1200 people. Disney is also well-known for its visitor services and attention to detail, making the system of interest for research on best practices in visitor transportation.

Designs for the original components of Disney World's transportation system were developed by Walt Disney himself; its monorail system and a network of ferryboats were part of a goal of allowing visitors to leave their cars parked throughout their stay. As the complex expanded in the 1980s, it became necessary to add a more conventional bus network to allow visitors to reach the new attractions, as expanding the monorail system was considered prohibitively expensive. Currently, the system comprises 263 buses, 12 ferryboats, and a 12-train monorail system.

The "Magic Kingdom" area of the complex is accessible only by Disney transportation, so all of its visitors use the system in some way. At the other parks and attractions, visitors are also permitted to use their own cars to get around, but in keeping with Mr. Disney's philosophy, the company makes strong efforts to encourage visitors to use the transportation system. In practical terms, this means providing transportation services that are frequent, easy to use, and free of charge. Specifically, vehicles are scheduled to arrive no more than 20 minutes apart, based on consumer research about acceptable waiting times. Waiting times can also be as short as 2½ minutes during peak periods on the monorail system. Walking distances to the stops are generally around 1200 feet, a

---

[19] The San Francisco Bay Area in particular has extensive transit coverage. Callers from outside the region can connect to 511 by dialing 510-817-1717.

[20] Orlando/Orange County CVB. http://www.orlandoinfo.com/cvbnew2/research/attraction_attendance

little less than one quarter-mile. The transportation system is also designed to be much more convenient than driving, since it allows visitors to be picked up and dropped off at hotel and attraction entrances rather than in remote parking areas.

Another key element of the effort to encourage use of the transportation system is providing information to guests. Brochures describing the transportation system are available at all of the on-site hotels, and the transit stops themselves are clearly marked. Guests may also pose questions about the transportation system to any staff member whenever they need assistance. Disney is exploring ways to provide transportation information via the in-room television systems at hotels and via kiosks at the parks. Another technology-based initiative is working to reduce scheduling problems and "bunching" on bus routes with the help of Global Positioning Systems and computer-assisted dispatching.

Disney transportation managers are aware that many of their visitors do not necessarily have positive associations with public transportation, and therefore they make efforts to highlight the entertaining and unique aspects of the system. Ferryboats are designed in turn-of-the-century themes and crew members sport nautical uniforms. The monorail has a futuristic "space age" theme, and operators sometimes permit visitors to ride up front with them at the controls. The monorail also has audio narration that provides a mixture of orientation, fun facts about the park, weather information, and tips on how to avoid long lines and have a more enjoyable visit. The buses, somewhat by contrast, are fairly standard transit-type models without any narration, though they are painted in a Disney color scheme and the company is exploring the addition of onboard audio systems.

Disney World no longer conducts separate visitor surveys solely on its transportation system, but it still collects extensive visitor feedback in a number of ways, including visitor surveys that include questions on the transportation system. These surveys have shown, not surprisingly, that visitors are much more pleased with the monorail and ferry services than with the bus services. Disney also views the survey data, letters from guests, and other forms of feedback as extremely valuable sources of insight. The company frequently uses this feedback to make adjustments to transit services and informational materials. For example, the brochures describing the transportation system were recently revised and simplified after visitors complained of being overwhelmed by the level of detail.

Implications for Washington
Orlando is a major tourist destination that has implemented a number of innovative solutions to the challenge of providing mobility to the millions of visitors who arrive each year. In evaluating these strategies, it is also important to remember the differences between Orlando and Washington, notably the diminished role of public transport and the way in which Orlando's tourism is spread across numerous self-contained theme parks and attractions rather than focused on a historic downtown.

The Lynx Lymmo downtown shuttle and the I-Ride Trolley are transit services that have become quite successful despite the generally unfavorable conditions for transit in Orlando. Both have garnered ridership by offering relatively *frequent service*, *low-cost fares*, and *attractive vehicles*, and by focusing their services on areas where there is a dense concentration of activities. I-Ride also points out how *public-private partnerships* and collaboration among stakeholders can be used to create services that both reduce congestion and improve the local business climate.

Orlando's 511 traveler information service is currently limited to traffic information for Interstate 4, so its value is fairly limited. However, a number of states and regions are developing – or have already deployed – *multimodal 511 systems* that also include information on transit services and other travel options. As 511 systems are launched nationwide, and as 511 becomes more and more familiar as the nationwide travel information phone number, it will become increasingly valuable to tourists seeking information on local transportation. No matter where in the country they travel, they will only need to dial 511 in order to access information on travel conditions and – ideally – to be connected to a live operator or automated system that can provide detailed public transit information.

The private transportation system at Disney World, while undoubtedly incorporating some of that company's "magic," is actually a good example of *getting the essentials right*: guests are strongly encouraged not to drive, and this exhortation is matched by service that is frequent, convenient, and free of charge. The transportation options also include elements of novelty and fun, and *informational materials and staff contact* are used to make visitors aware of their options. Disney also *actively solicits feedback* from visitors and ensures that its services are adjusted in response.

Orlando: Summary of effective practices
General strategies:
Provide a free or low-cost downtown shuttle with frequent service and attractive vehicles
Use public-private partnerships as a funding source for visitor-oriented transit services
Create a multimodal traveler information system
For sightseeing or visitor transportation services:
Use staff contact and informational materials to promote encourage use of ATS rather than driving
Use ongoing customer feedback to improve services

PHILADELPHIA

The context

Philadelphia is home to 1.5 million people, with 6.2 million in the metropolitan area as a whole. Its importance to American history was cemented by the signing of the Declaration of Independence and Constitution, as well as the city's stint as the nation's capital from 1790 to 1800. Many visitors are drawn to the city by an interest in American history and the Revolutionary period, with major sights including Independence Hall, the Liberty Bell, and Old City Hall. Others are attracted by the city's diverse, lively neighborhoods, its museums of art and culture, and its many famous arboretums and gardens. The Philadelphia region hosted 11.2 million overnight visitors in 2001[21].

Traffic congestion in Philadelphia is not as severe as in Washington or Boston; the region's Travel Time Index was 1.30 in 2001, making it only the 27th-worst in the country overall[22]. Nonetheless, the center city area can be quite congested, and public-private partnerships and civic groups such as the Central Philadelphia Development Corporation have been working to promote the awareness and use of transit in center city, as the downtown area is known.

Public transportation

The Southeastern Pennsylvania Transit Authority (SEPTA) is the main agency responsible for public transportation in region. SEPTA's services include buses, trolleys, above- and below-ground trains, and regional rail services fanning outward into the suburbs. The services that visitors are likely to find most useful are the Market-Frankford and Broad Street subway lines, the LUCY (Loop through University City) bus,

---

[21] Philadelphia Convention and Visitors Bureau.
[22] Texas Transportation Institute, Urban Mobility Study.

and bus route 38, which links Independence Hall to a number of museums and hotels. The R1 rail line also provides service to the airport. All in all, the SEPTA system provides access to nearly all of the major visitor attractions of Philadelphia. Day Passes – originally marketed to tourists, but now also used by many locals – sell for $5.50 and allow unlimited rides on local transit services, plus a one-way ride on any of the regional rail lines. Even if the regional rail trip is not used, the Day Pass can provide significant value over the standard one-way SEPTA fare of $2.

For visitors traveling to or from the New Jersey suburbs, the Delaware River Port Authority's PATCO Speedline provides frequent, inexpensive train service to center city Philadelphia. Tickets cost between $1.45 and $2.45, with the option of a discounted transfer to SEPTA services in center city. Most of the stations on the New Jersey side also have free parking, making the Speedline a useful park-and-ride option for day-trippers coming from New Jersey.

Tourist transportation management strategies
Like Boston and Savannah, Philadelphia has had to take action to regulate the flow of tour buses in its downtown area. At the very center of the city, Independence National Historic Park sees the arrival of as many as 60 tour buses per hour during peak periods. In response to the traffic congestion, noise, and exhaust problems caused by these buses, the NPS has worked together with the City of Philadelphia and other stakeholders to create a plan for managing these bus flows. Central to these plans was to consolidate all bus loading and unloading into the newly built Independence Transportation Center, which is adjacent to the Independence Visitor Center. A bus parking and layover facility was also established several blocks away, where drivers can park their buses and rest in waiting rooms (complete with showers and sleeping areas) until their pick-up times for the return trip[23]. Bus parking at this facility is $20, or $30 for overnight parking. With the new facility in place, the city has stressed that regulations against stopping and idling on nearby streets would be strictly enforced.

Philadelphia's efforts to provide information and orientation to visitors have also been boosted by the advent of the Independence Visitor Center, which is in center city near Independence Hall. This center is the result of a complex partnership arrangement between the city and state governments, tourism promotion authorities, the NPS, and a number of other public agencies and charitable trusts. It is run by Independence Visitor Center Corporation, an independent non-profit organization established for this purpose. It serves as the primary point of orientation for Independence National Historical Park as well as for the city of Philadelphia, four surrounding counties, and the Delaware River front in New Jersey. The center is at or near the starting point for several private sightseeing services and a SEPTA stop; an on-site garage parking is also available so that visitors can leave their cars for the day while they explore Philadelphia. As such the center illustrates how orientation can be co-located with a hub for visitor transportation.

---

[23] Volpe Center, Tour Bus Management Initiative Best Practices Report. For additional details, see Volpe Center study, Evaluation of Bus Management Options for the Independence National Historic Park, May 18, 2000.

Since 1994, the City of Philadelphia has also sponsored the Phlash, a visitor-oriented bus service. The Phlash's distinctive buses – painted deep purple with a turquoise wing logo – make a 12-stop loop of the center city area, departing from the Independence Visitor Center every 10-15 minutes and providing access to roughly 40 places of interest and 8,000 hotel rooms. The service is operated by SEPTA under contract with the city; rides are $1 each way. The Phlash has proven popular with visitors and with some residents, carrying 30,000 passengers in the summer of 2002. (Since then, however, budgetary considerations have led to talk of its elimination, and its future is uncertain.[24])

Philadelphia's tourism agencies also promote the use of SEPTA transit services and encourage visitors to walk throughout the compact center city area. The Greater Philadelphia Tourism Marketing Corporation proudly describes Philadelphia as a walking city, and the transportation-related section of its Philadelphia Trip Planner includes walking guides and a map entitled "Getting Around: A Walker's Delight."[25] Other tourism-promotion agencies have similar messages and promote walking and transit in their suggested tours and itineraries.

Private transportation and tours

Philadelphia has a number of hop-on/hop-off tours that are roughly similar in approach. The Big Bus Company offers a 90-minute narrated tour of the city center, stopping at the major sites such as the US Mint, Independence Hall, City Hall, and the Academy of Fine Art. The tour uses British-style double-decker buses that are open-topped in summer; narration is provided by a separate guide rather than the driver. A 24-hour pass with off-and-on privileges is $25. Philadelphia Trolley Tours offers a similar service using Victorian-style trolley buses, with a 90-minute, 18-stop tour covering largely the same area of the city center, with driver-provided narration. Tickets are $20 and include all-day on-and-off privileges plus the option of a separate 40-minute excursion to Fairmount Park. Both companies send vehicles roughly every half-hour during the summer peak and reduce the frequencies slightly in winter.

One factor worth mentioning is that while Big Bus' double-deckers are distinctive and afford visitors a unique vantage point on the city from their upper level, they are not accessible to those with disabilities. Some, but not all, of Philadelphia Trolley Tours' vehicles are accessible. Both tours start near the intersection of 5th and Market Streets and are thus within easy reach (less than one block) of both a subway station and the parking facility at the Independence Visitor Center. Both tours also mark the stops along the way with distinctive signage. In a number of cases these stops are co-located with SEPTA public bus stops; for instance, 10 out of the 20 Big Bus stops are also SEPTA stops, but are marked with a star-shaped logo to distinguish them.

The Big Bus Tour also includes a stop at 30th Street Station. This is an important connection, because 30th Street Station provides access not only to local and regional

[24] Philadelphia Inquirer. http://www.philly.com/mld/philly/news/local/6214320.htm
[25] On-line version of the map at http://www.gophila.com/gettinghere/walkersdelightmap.htm.

SEPTA transit services, but to Amtrak trains and New Jersey Transit as well. Travelers coming into Philadelphia by train for a daytrip – either from a suburban park-and-ride station or from other cities on the east coast – can thus join the tour without worrying about additional travel connections. This again reinforces the incentive to travel to Philadelphia without a car and to use public transportation and other ATS throughout one's visit.

The Philadelphia Duck Tours are similar to those in Boston, with an 80-minute narrated tour provided via amphibious vehicles. The Philadelphia tour departs from the area around Independence Hall, and is thus accessible both to SEPTA transit services and to the parking facility at the Independence Visitor Center.   The Duck Tour takes visitors around the historical sites of center city, to Society Hill and Penn's Landing, and into the Delaware River. Tickets are $20, and the vehicles are accessible to travelers with disabilities.

Implications for Washington
Philadelphia employs a mix of strategies to manage visitor transportation. Perhaps the best-known initiative is the establishment of the Independence Visitor Center and Independence Transportation Center. These facilities are good examples of the value of *working with public- and private-sector stakeholders* to find mutually beneficial solutions to the problems posed by visitor transportation. This collaboration has created a rational system for tour bus drop-offs, pick-ups, and layovers. The center is also something of a *gateway* for visitors arriving by car, with tourist information brochures providing driving directions to the visitor center, where these travelers can park their car, gather orientation materials, and continue on foot or by transit.

The city and its tourism agencies have also made efforts to promote walking and public transportation, particularly with *walking-oriented orientation and marketing materials* such as the Walker's Delight map. The local transit agency has aided this effort with *public transit passes* that offer good value and are valid on all modes of local travel. Another benefit to SEPTA's day passes is that they include a ride on the suburban rail network, encouraging visitors to venture beyond the typical tourist circuit of center city to take in some of the sites of the broader region.

Philadelphia also runs a *bus loop* known as the Phlash to provide visitor transportation to the main sites of center city and to hotels and restaurants, thus reducing the need for visitors to take their own cars. Like other successful visitor-oriented transit services, the Phlash offers frequent service and has distinctive markings that differentiate it from other transit services.

The major visitor transportation and sightseeing services in Philadelphia also use vehicles that are *visually distinctive* – double-decker buses, vintage-style trolleys, amphibious "ducks" – and the narrated tours remain popular despite the availability of the inexpensive Phlash bus service.   These sightseeing services connect to local SEPTA services at multiple points, particularly the Market-Frankford line's subway stop at 5th and Market Streets in the heart of the historic district.   They can also be accessed from commercial parking facilities, including the one at the Independence Visitor Center and eight other garages within a few blocks of the center. The Big Bus Tour also links to SEPTA regional rail, Amtrak, and New Jersey transit via its stop at 30th Street Station. These kinds of *intermodal connections* permit easy transfers to visitor transportation and sightseeing services and make it more convenient to use suburban park-and-ride facilities for the trip into the city.

Philadelphia: Summary of effective practices
General strategies:
Provide a free or low-cost visitor shuttle
Work with other stakeholders to find common solutions to parking and transportation problems
Establish a visitor center to provide orientation
Encourage walking and transit use with walking maps and discounted transit passes
For sightseeing and visitor transportation services:
Use visually distinctive vehicles
Provide connections to local transit stops and intermodal connection points

LONDON

The context

From its beginnings as a small Roman fortification, London has grown into a major world city, the capital of the United Kingdom and its (substantially smaller but still far-flung) empire, and – most importantly for the purposes of this report – a popular tourist destination. Figures from 2002 indicate that 28 million people visited the city for at least one night[26]. About 76% of overseas visitors come for leisure and 21% are from the United States. Many of London's leisure visitors are drawn by the city's famous landmarks, such as Westminster Abbey, Buckingham Palace, and the Tower of London, as well as by the city's world-class museums of history and art, including the British Museum, Victoria & Albert Museum, and National Gallery. Others are drawn by the city's nightlife, fashion, and cultural scenes, as epitomized by the government's recent "Cool Britannia" slogan.

London itself – i.e., the area covered by the Greater London Authority (GLA), the regional governmental body with responsibilities for the 33 London boroughs[27] – is home to 7.2 million people.[28] This figure rises to nearly 14 million when the suburban areas of the Home Counties are also included[29]. Though comparable mobility data are not available, London's traffic congestion problems are commensurate with what would be expected of a metropolitan area of this size, and traffic speeds in the inner London area average less than 10 miles per hour[30].

In an attempt to reduce this congestion and to provide revenues for improving public transportation, the GLA introduced a "congestion charging" program in February 2003. This program imposes a charge of £5 (roughly $8.90) on almost all private vehicles entering a 22 square kilometer area of central London between 7 am and 6:30 pm weekdays[31]. So far, the charging policy has worked with a minimum of technical glitches, and is credited with reducing traffic congestion within the charging zone by about 30 percent (without increasing congestion outside of the zone).

---

[26] Visit London (formerly known as the London Tourist Board and Convention Bureau).

[27] By way of background, the GLA is a regional government with responsibility for issues that are inherently regional in scope, such as land-use planning, transportation, economic development, and emergency services. Other local functions are handled at the level of the individual London boroughs. One of the GLA's main responsibilities is to oversee Transport for London (TfL), the public transportation agency.

[28] 2001 UK Census.

[29] http://www.demographia.com/db-lon9101 htm

[30] Transport for London, http://www.tfl.gov.uk/tfl/abt_tfl.shtml

[31] The details of the program are complex, but essentially, drivers who enter the charging area are responsible for adding their license plate number to a database beforehand, or no later than 10pm on the day of travel. This transaction can be done by phone, internet, mobile phone text message, or via a newsagent or retail shop. The charge is then enforced through a network of traffic cameras and mobile enforcement vans, which compare vehicle license plates against those registered in the database. There is a £40 ($71) fine for violations. The program also allows for a number of discounts (e.g. for residents of the zone and alternative-fuel vehicles) as well as total exemptions for licensed taxis, transit vehicles, emergency vehicles, the armed forces, and a handful of other special categories.

Enforcing this charge requires a complex network of computer systems, video cameras, enforcement patrols, and customer-service call centers; most of these operational aspects have been contracted out to a private firm. According to the most recent estimates[32], the charge will bring in £165 million ($295 million) in gross revenues during its first year of operation, though £97 million ($173 million) of this will be consumed by administrative expenses. However, this still yields net revenues of £68 million ($121 million) per year, a figure that is expected to rise over time to £80 or £100 million ($143 to $179 million) per year as start-up costs are paid down. By law, all of the proceeds from the charge must be dedicated to public transit improvements.

Public transportation
London has an extremely comprehensive public transportation network that includes underground (subway), bus, and light-rail services, plus suburban and national rail lines and two Thames river services. The underground system is the world's oldest; it includes 12 lines, 329 km of track, and 275 stations, and carries 3 million passengers each day. The bus system is one of the most extensive urban systems in the world, with 6500 buses running on hundreds of routes and carrying roughly 4.5 million passengers each day. Underground services run every few minutes and major bus routes run every 5-10 minutes weekdays. Between midnight and 5 a.m., underground services are replaced by special "night bus" routes that fan out from Trafalgar Square.

Nearly all of London's major visitor attractions are easily accessible by underground or bus, generally by multiple routes, and the system's overall convenience makes it very attractive to visitors. (This is especially true when considered in light of the high cost of driving and parking in London. On top of the new congestion charge, daily parking charges in central London garages can top £20 or even £25 [$36-$45].) Every major travel guide to London recommends using public transportation, and this message is reinforced in trip-planning brochures, orientation materials, and transit system maps and signage.

Transport for London (TfL) offers a number of visitor-oriented daily passes such as the One-Day Travelcard. Among the options is a discounted card for those willing to wait until after 9:30 a.m. to travel on weekdays, and a Family Travelcard that offers a discounted rate for adults and children traveling together. As a further service to visitors, Transport for London is studying the possibility of accepting foreign currency (the Euro) at ticket machines in major international arrival stations such as Heathrow Airport and Waterloo railway station (where the Eurostar cross-Channel services arrive).

Tourist transportation management strategies
Managing tour bus traffic is particularly important in London, with its congested network of narrow streets. Two local authorities in the heart of the city, the City of Westminster and the Corporation of London, have implemented a number of strategies for managing tour bus traffic. In Westminster, a total of 53 on-street coach parking spaces are made

---

[32] Transport for London. *Congestion Charging: Six Months On.* October 2003.

available in high-traffic areas, but parking meters are in effect to promote expeditious use and turnover of spaces. The metering is enforced from 8:30 am to 6:30 pm weekdays and from 8:30 am to 1:30 pm on Saturdays; the rate is £4 ($7.15) per hour. In the City of London, coach parking is prohibited except for three designated areas, where charges in the range of £3-5 ($5.35-8.90) per hour are in effect. At the busiest site, the Tower of London, tour buses are charged £10 ($17.85) for the first hour and £6 ($10.70) per hour thereafter during the summer peak season. In both boroughs, bus parking is banned overnight and illegal bus parking, e.g. outside of a designated bay, is subject to a stiff £50 ($89) fine, which rises to £100 ($179) if not paid within 14 days.

At the regional level, the Greater London Authority has been working to improve the quality of public transportation, particularly on the bus system. The GLA's strategies include increasing the number of dedicated bus lanes, strictly enforcing no-parking rules on bus priority routes, installing traffic-signal priority equipment for buses, and providing estimated waiting times to passengers via electronic message boards at bus stops. TfL has also been working to make it easier for less familiar riders to use the bus system, by posting "spider" maps at bus stops (see example below), showing bus routes in a way that resembles subway maps, with clearly marked lines and stops.

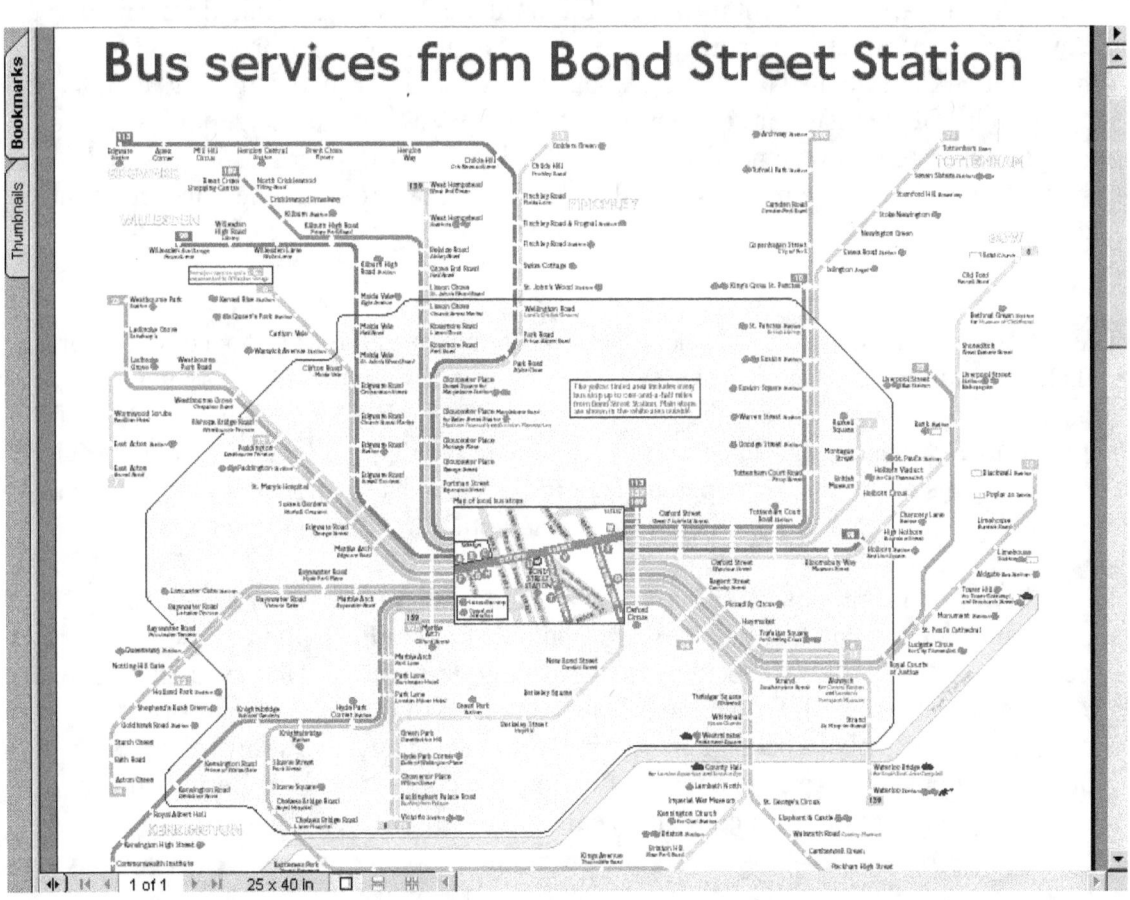

The idea of promoting the use of public transportation via information and marketing has been raised to an art form in London. The TfL website, for example, includes the following useful features:

- "Visiting London", a four-page travel guide, available in 13 languages, that includes visitor-oriented information about services and fares, plus a map of the underground system and a detailed street and bus route map of central London. The guide is formatted so that visitors can easily print it out and take it with them[33].
- A Journey Planner that prepares complete bus and underground itineraries based on the user's origin, destination, and time of travel[34].
- An interactive, clickable underground map that shows bus connections and the local area around each station[35]. (The maps also show the *exact* locations of the Tube exits and bus stops. This is an important feature for less-familiar travelers, especially since many underground stations have multiple exits and connect to dozens of bus routes at multiple street-level stops.)

These services all come together in an amazingly comprehensive website module called "Tube Guru."[36] Tube Guru combines interactive maps of the city and underground system with updates on current travel conditions and delays, plus detailed information on the availability of street-level amenities like ATMs, public toilets, parking, and taxis. What is remarkable about Tube Guru is that, for each underground station, it also provides a list of the visitor attractions, street markets, restaurants, bars, pubs, clubs, and other nightlife spots that are nearby, often with editorial reviews and user-provided commentary. The service promotes public transit both by providing detailed information and (more subtly) by using underground stations as its primary point of reference and orientation.

The official tourist board, Visit London (formerly known as the London Tourist Board and Convention Bureau), also provides information for prospective visitors via a sophisticated online presence. The "getting around" page includes a link straight to TfL's online journey planner, plus a pan-and-zoom interactive map of the city with 37,000 clickable points of interest. A separate page provides updated information on traffic and transit delays, road closures and construction, and other travel conditions.

The utility of online modules like Tube Guru and the Visit London map is currently somewhat limited by the fact that they are available only online, whereas most visitors have limited internet access once they arrive at their destination. However, these services are laying the groundwork for a comprehensive system of online visitor information, something that is likely to become increasingly important and useful over the next few years, as handheld and wireless devices with internet connections proliferate. It is not hard to imagine a world in which tourists equipped with internet-capable cellphones or

---

[33] http://www.tfl.gov.uk/tfl/vlt_guide.shtml
[34] http://journeyplanner.tfl.gov.uk/
[35] http://map.tfl.gov.uk/map.asp
[36] http://tube.tfl.gov.uk/guru/index.asp

other wireless internet gadgets would make full use of online services in order to navigate unfamiliar cities and public transportation systems.

Of course, human interaction will always be an important part of visitor orientation, and TfL and Visit London do not limit themselves to online activities. The two organizations operate a network of information centers throughout London. TfL has 11 Traveler Information Centers, located mostly in major underground stations, and Visit London has an additional 13 Tourist Information Centers located throughout the city. It is worth noting that several of the centers are located at major intermodal stations, including Heathrow Airport, Waterloo railway station, and Victoria coach station, so visitors can begin receiving information upon arrival in the city.

TfL also works with the *London Pass* program, which bundles a public transportation pass together with a card that provides free admission to dozens of London museums and attractions. Other benefits to the pass include discounts on sightseeing tours, discounted theatre and cinema admissions, and the ability to "jump the queue" at some busy attractions. Passes are available for 1-, 2-, 3-, and 6-day periods. A one-day pass sells for about £32 ($57) and a 6-day pass is about £110 ($197), so they represent best value for those who plan on packing many museum visits and activities into their days. (Indeed, the promoters of the pass point out that visiting all of the sites to which the card offers admission would cost over £400 [$715].)

Private transportation and tours
Bus tours: The Big Bus Company (an affiliate of the Philadelphia service described above) and The Original Tour both run narrated, hop-on/hop-off tours of London's major sights using double-decker buses. These buses are not accessible to those with disabilities, even on the lower level. Otherwise, the services are similar to those offered in Boston, Savannah, and Philadelphia, though there are more options for recorded foreign-language commentary. Another interesting difference is that each company operates multiple routes (3 routes on Big Bus, 5 routes on The Original Tour) that are included in the price of a single ticket. These routes include the usual sightseeing loops plus connecting routes that provide service to specific points of interest or hotel districts; they are generally geared to geographic corridors rather than thematic interests. All the same, the existence of multiple routes allows visitors to mix and match the tours as they wish, connecting between different tour routes and creating more individualized itineraries. Buses generally depart every 10 to 15 minutes on the main sightseeing routes and every 20-25 minutes on the "connector" routes. Tickets are valid all day and cost £17 ($30) on Big Bus and £15 ($27) on The Original Tour. Big Bus tours also include a 90-minute guided walking tour of sites around London, geared to themes such as the British monarchy, London's ghosts, and rock-and-roll music. These tours are free with the price of a Big Bus ticket and are offered at a fee to others.

In addition to providing connecting service to hotel districts, both companies make it easy for visitors to connect to the tour from public transportation, with many of the departure points located adjacent to underground stations. Their websites and brochures also offer information on joining the tour directly from London's airports and major railway stations. Connections to parking facilities are a bit more complicated given the physical layout of London, but TfL makes parking available at a number of outlying underground stations, generally for about £2-3 ($3.50-$5.35) per day (free on Sundays and holidays).

Big Bus tours are coordinated with a sightseeing cruise on the Thames; a 30-minute riverboat trip is included in the price of the day's bus ticket. The Original Tour, for its part, offers an innovative interpretive option: children are provided with a Kid's Club activity pack (geared toward ages 5 to 12) that allows children to follow along with the tour and gather the answer to questions about London while also completing drawing and coloring activities.

Taxi tours: London is well-known for its distinctive black taxicabs and the rigorous examinations that cabdrivers must pass before becoming licensed. Black Taxi Tours of London leverages these attributes by offering tours of London that are led and narrated by licensed drivers. The standard tour is a 2-hour loop covering the Tower of London, Parliament, and other top attractions, but visitors are also free to choose from a set of thematic tours or to request their own preferred set of destinations. Indeed, the company markets its tours as a flexible, fun alternative to the large bus tours, with commentary that is also perhaps more insightful and "unofficial". Tours begin and end at the visitor's hotel or other preferred location, making door-to-door service another attractive feature. This convenience comes at a price, of course, with the two-hour tours costing £75 ($134) per carload (£85 [$152] at night). However, the taxis can accommodate up to 5 people, so this may be a reasonably economical option for larger groups.

Bicycle tours:
The London Bicycle Tour Company offers three different bicycle-based tours, each focusing on a particular section of London. The tours are led by a guide who cycles along with the group and provides interpretation at stops along the way. The tours are offered once a week or on request, and are 6 to 9 miles in length and 3 to 3½ hours in duration. The price of £15 ($27) includes insurance and a helmet; bicycle rental (for those who require it) is arranged through their rental shop for an additional £2.50 ($4.50) per hour or £12 ($21) per day. The company also designs special tours for groups with a particular thematic interest, such as architecture or Charles Dickens.

River tours:
At least eight different companies operate sightseeing cruises on the Thames River. Some of these head upstream to the Royal Botanical Gardens at Kew and to Hampton Court Palace, while others travel downstream to Greenwich, which is home to the Royal Observatory and the National Maritime Museum. Of particular interest here is the "hop-on, hop-off circular cruise" offered by Crown River Cruises. This service calls at 24 different stops along the banks of the river, including major destinations such as the Houses of Parliament, the Tate Modern Gallery, Globe Theatre, and Tower of London. Passengers are free either to stay aboard for a full circuit or to hop off at any point and re-board later. In practice, the ability to hop on and off is much greater in the peak summer

season, when boats run every 30 minutes; frequencies are reduced to every 40 minutes during spring and fall, and every 80 minutes during the winter. Tickets are £6.20 ($11).

Implications for Washington

London has both a strong public transportation network and an array of private tour services operating across multiple modes of travel. The city's efforts to control visitor traffic and promote the use of ATS are two-pronged: they promote and facilitate the use of public transportation, while also instituting policies that make travel by private car more expensive and less convenient.

The political climate and governmental structure of London differs from that of Washington in several important respects, and it is therefore unlikely that a daily congestion charge, or other measure that would significantly raise the cost of car travel, would be implemented in the near term. Nonetheless, the NPS can take certain steps that are under its control, such as reducing the amount of free parking in NPS lots, while it works with local governments on longer-term solutions to the congestion problem. The NPS can also adopt some of London's strategies that make public transportation and other ATS more attractive and convenient, such as:

- Working with public transit agencies, tourist boards, and local governments to present a coordinated message to visitors about the convenience of transit, including a sophisticated online presence and a physical presence at major intermodal stations
- Examining innovative ideas such as bundling public transit passes with museum admission cards.

London's diversity of private tour services also reinforces the idea of meeting visitors' desires for more and more options for travel modes and themes, and particularly their preference for tours that allow greater individuality and customization. Even the conventional sightseeing tours offer multiple overlapping routes so that visitors can essentially design their own tours, and one also includes a choice of thematic walking tours around the city. Again, while the NPS is unlikely to get into the business of providing tours via every conceivable mode of travel, it is worth considering the value of additional options when designing the structure of visitor transportation services.

London: Summary of effective practices
General strategies:
Mitigate congestion via roadway charging and investment in transit
Employ a mixture of regulation and accommodation to handle tour buses
Create a multi-layered system of visitor information and public transit information, including a sophisticated internet presence
Consider bundling a transit pass with museum admissions
For sightseeing and visitor transportation services:
Offer multiple interconnecting routes, add-on walking tours, or other ways for increased customization of itineraries
Provide connections to local transit stops and intermodal connection points
Use vehicles that are icons of the city or appropriate to their setting

IV. CONCLUSIONS

In a city as large and complex as Washington, there will be no one single strategy that will address all of the issues presented by visitor transportation. There are also limits to the extent to which strategies employed by other cities will be directly transferable to Washington. Nonetheless, the experiences of Boston, Savannah, Orlando, Philadelphia, and London all suggest possible strategies that Washington could adopt to its benefit. This section summarizes these strategies, starting with general approaches for managing visitor transportation and then moving on to specific recommendations for the Washington visitor transportation services.

General transportation management strategies

Collaborate with other stakeholders:

The five cities studied here have, in one way or another, all promoted coordination between the city government, public agencies, and other stakeholders to work together on issues related to visitor transportation. This should be a key element of any strategy for central Washington as well. In fact, because the city's diverse activities and institutional complexity limit the ability of the NPS to effect changes on its own, coordinated solutions will prove more effective.

One approach that seems particularly relevant to Washington is Boston's idea of convening a multi-stakeholder **Tourism Transportation Task Force** to develop and weigh proposals for improving visitor transportation. For Washington and the National Mall and surrounding park areas, such a task force could bring together the NPS, the DC Department of Transportation (DDOT), the Washington Convention and Visitors Bureau, representatives from the travel and tourism industry, the Washington Metropolitan Area Transit Authority (WMATA), museums and historical groups, and Advisory Neighborhood Councils[37]. The goal would be to work collaboratively to find solutions that serve tourists, residents, and businesses alike. Specific proposals might include changes to curbside management policies or transit services, or a public-private collaboration to produce a **visitor card** that combines a WMATA pass with discounted (or queue-jumping) admission to museums and historic sites and/or tickets to a visitor transportation service or sightseeing tour. Whatever the specific proposals, the task force would provide a mechanism for **information exchange** and collaborative problem-solving.

---

[37] A group with a more regional focus might also include the Metropolitan Washington Council of Government, the National Capital Planning Commission, and local authorities in neighboring cities and counties in Maryland and Virginia.

Leverage existing assets by providing more public transit information:

Washington is fortunate to have an efficient, comprehensive public transportation network, so visitors would benefit from **improved information and trip-planning assistance**. London, another city with an extensive public transportation network, provides a good example of how existing transit services can be complemented by an impressive array of in-person and online visitor information. TfL information centers are located at busy stations throughout the city, including important visitor hubs such as Heathrow Airport and Waterloo Station. Meanwhile, the official Visit London webpage links directly to TfL's online door-to-door itinerary planning service. TfL's website also provides detailed interactive maps, tips for visitors, and a range of much more detailed information such as reviews of restaurants near transit stops and the locations of ATMs and public toilets.

Implementing these kinds of improvements and sophisticated online services would require working with WMATA to **increase distribution of transit maps and schedules** and to add **specific visitor-oriented modules to the WMATA website**. The NPS could also work closely with WMATA and with the Departments of Transportation in DC, Maryland, and Virginia to ensure that public transit information will have a high-profile presence on any **regional 511 telephone information system** that is developed. Out-of-town tourists generally do not know the relevant local phone numbers for transit and traffic information, or even what services might be available. As 511 becomes a nationwide service, however, increasingly they will be familiar with 511 as the number to dial, connecting them to local travel information wherever they happen to be. It will therefore be valuable to have transit information – and ideally, specific information about visitor transportation services and travel – available through any future 511 system developed for the region. A possible first step could be the ability to be transferred directly from 511 to WMATA's existing itinerary-planning call center, allowing transit trips to be planned more easily.

In terms of steps that the NPS can take on its own, much can be done to **augment the level of transit information on NPS websites**. In fact, a quick review of the travel-planning information on the websites of NPS units in and around central Washington showed that transit directions are sometimes missing altogether. When transit directions are present, they are usually listed last, and then with just with a general description, e.g.:

> There are several metro train routes from the suburban areas surrounding the city. The Foggy Bottom metro station is the closest stop to the Lincoln Memorial.

At a minimum, a direct link to WMATA's online itinerary planner could be provided on the pages that do not have one already. Additional information might include background information on the transit system (first and last trains, typical service frequencies, fare payment, safety, convenience) as well as walking directions from the nearest Metrorail or Metrobus stop. The sections on air travel to Washington could also include details on using public transportation services to reach Washington from the region's three airports. As it stands now, most NPS sites and even the website of the Convention and Visitors Bureau have only limited information on taking public transit to and from the airports. This is particularly important in light of research indicating that **information about transit service at airports** and rail terminals is particularly influential in visitors' decisions to take public transit[38].

In short, the current level of transit information is limited enough that prospective visitors to Washington could be forgiven for thinking that they might need a car throughout their stay – for the trip from the airport, for getting to the major monuments or other sites of personal interest, for sampling the city's restaurants and nightlife. The NPS websites, and ideally those of WMATA as well, should strongly counter that view by providing as much detailed visitor-oriented public transit information as possible. It would also be useful to take London's example of a **layered approach to transit information**, offering materials that range from a basic print-and-go overview of transit services to the most detailed interactive online modules, so that prospective visitors can receive the mix of information that is most useful to them. Basic pre-trip planning information should be the near-term priority, while more sophisticated services will be increasingly important as demand for **online information accessible by wireless internet** rises over time.

Another potentially fruitful approach would involve working with WMATA to **craft transit passes to visitors' needs**. Allowing a single pass to be valid on both bus and rail services, and possibly with the NPS sightseeing services as well, would be one simple but useful step in helping visitors to make the most of the transit system. London's off-peak discount for travel after 9:30 a.m. presents an example of how a valuable discount can be provided without adding to the crowding on peak-hour services. Another idea worth borrowing is that of having the pass include, as in Philadelphia, a ride on a regional rail service, so that visitors have some encouragement to explore the broader region. This would involve working together with the Maryland and Virginia commuter-rail systems, MARC and VRE.

Promote walking and bicycling:

Given the proximity of many of the monuments and museums to one another, it is not surprising that walking is already the most typical mode of transportation between attractions in central Washington[39]. It is still worthwhile to promote walking, since this is a non-polluting mode of transportation and an excellent way for visitors to get a feel for the city at their own pace. The ability to increase pedestrian mode share is limited by the fact that many individual travelers will prefer not to walk, due to factors such as disability, distance, and weather conditions. Overall, though, certain strategies to promote walking can be effective. These would include working together with the District and with tourism promotion authorities to provide more **walking-scale maps**, such as the Philadelphia map that celebrates the joys of walking in the city. Tourism marketing materials can also take a page from Savannah, where colorful prose is used to describe walking as the ideal way to tour the city and soak up its charms. Boston's

---

[38] Slabic, Cristina Borja, "The role of advanced technology in facilitating transit use for tourists." Texas A&M University, August 1997.
[39] NPS, Washington, DC Visitor Survey.

Freedom Trail, while likely not an exact model for Washington, points out the value of having **street-level information that is explicitly pedestrian-oriented**, such as directional signs, blazes, and kiosk maps. All in all, the National Mall area is currently a very walkable environment, and this pedestrian-friendliness should be appropriately expanded and promoted as part of a larger atmosphere of pedestrian visitor destinations in the downtown area.

Like walking, bicycling is not practical or convenient for all travelers, but it is a zero-emission form of transportation that should be encouraged as much as possible. In addition, as the bicycle tours in Savannah and London suggest, bicycling seems to be gaining popularity as a form of visitor transportation – unsurprisingly so, since it is relatively inexpensive and provides independent mobility, aerobic exercise, an ability to set one's own schedule, and a unique perspective on the city and region. In terms of practical steps to support cycling, the NPS could supply more **bike parking**; add **bike racks** to sightseeing vehicles; use **wayfinding signage** to guide cyclists between destinations; provide **pre-trip information**, such as route guidance and bike parking information, on its websites and in its brochures; and continue to promote and improve **multi-modal trail uses**.

Incorporate transit buses into the mix and/or consider shuttle services:

In addition to the NPS visitor transportation system, walking, biking, and/or driving, many visitors also use the Metrorail system, and surveys indicate that they find Metrorail easy to use.[40] There are many monuments, memorials, and park sites, however, that are beyond easy walking distance of Metrorail stations. The Jefferson Memorial, for example, is nine-tenths of a mile from the nearest station, well beyond the quarter-mile distance that was suggested by the Boston case study. In these cases, **transit buses** can be a valuable complement to subway services, providing connections to and from stations. However, tourists tend to find the bus system less easy to use than subways[41]. This is an area where coordination with WMATA and other partners could be fruitful, potentially leading to the development of additional Metrobus routes serving areas near the Mall and providing connections to Metrorail stations.

Better information provision would help, too, as visitors are often unaware of the bus options that are available to them. To give one example, numerous respondents in the visitor survey listed the Washington National Cathedral as a site that they were unable to visit because it is not accessible by transit. In fact, the Cathedral is served by fairly frequent bus routes on the Wisconsin Avenue and Massachusetts Avenue lines (routes 30, 32, 34, 35, 36, N2, N3, N4, and N6).

---

[40] NPS, Washington, DC Visitor Survey.
[41] NPS, Washington, DC Visitor Survey. The survey also found that visitors are slightly less comfortable with bus services and less likely to find them easy to use (60% described buses as "easy" or "very easy," compared to 90% for Metrorail).

Again, one easy step toward encouraging bus use would be to offer transit passes that are valid on both subways and buses, as is done in Boston, Philadelphia, and London. This reduces the guesswork associated with buses and the need to carry exact change, and reinforces the idea of a coordinated multimodal system. Better bus information, such as London's **detailed maps of stops and "spider" route maps** can also be provided in information brochures and at bus stops themselves to help "demystify" the bus system. A recent *Washington Post* article on improving bus service also mentioned strategies such as prepaid fare cards, better parking enforcement at bus stops, the construction of bus-only corridors, and the provision of real-time information to passengers,[42] all of which would of course need to be coordinated with WMATA, DDOT, and other stakeholders.

A separate but related innovation would be a **shuttle route** or other service that would serve residents and tourists alike. These shuttles have proven popular in Savannah, Orlando, and Philadelphia. Though each service is different, key factors for success include **frequent service, reduced or free fares, and service that is enhanced through the use of dedicated transit lanes and/or traffic-signal priority**[43]. Another common thread is using colorful stops and buses to create a **distinctive look**, reinforcing the idea that the shuttle service is somewhat separate from the rest of the transit system and making it easier to identify in a busy urban environment.

Consider a range of transportation demand management strategies to deal with cars and tour buses:

As described in the preceding sections, London has had great success with its daily congestion charge, which has relieved traffic congestion in the center of the city while also generating revenue for improving public transportation. Savannah has instituted a strict regime of regulation of tourist transportation services, and Boston and Philadelphia have instituted measures to manage tour bus traffic. Each of these strategies is a response to the specific transportation needs and political realities of the city in question, so there are limits to their transferability. The broader point is that there can be great rewards to refining the **mixture of carrots and sticks that a city uses to influence transportation decisions**. In particular, the experiences of the case-study cities are evidence that imposing traffic controls and additional costs on car and bus travel – when structured properly as part of a balanced program – do not erode a city's commercial vitality or its popularity as a tourist destination. On the contrary, such programs can improve overall traffic flow and mobility and improve the visitor experience. An early review of London's congestion charge, for instance, showed that the impact of the program on retail traffic was quite minor, and that the overall benefits of the program (particularly improved mobility and journey-time reliability) outweighed the costs by some £50 million ($89 million) per year[44].

---

[42] Layton, Lyndsey. "Turning Back to the Humble Bus," Washington Post, B1, Nov. 25, 2003.
[43] See the DC Downtown Circulator Plan for more discussion of the services that have been proposed. www.downtowndc.org
[44] Transport for London. *Congestion Charging: Six Months On.* October 2003.

One of the most fundamental steps the NPS can take to manage transportation demand is to consider **establishing parking fees** in areas within the core of Washington, for example near the Mall and on Ohio Drive SW. Higher parking fees reduce the attractiveness of driving into central Washington and reinforce the messages about walking, bicycling, and public transit. Higher meter rates will also increase the turnover of parking spaces for those who continue to drive, reducing the unnecessary driving that is caused by circling around for on-street parking spaces. The **"pay-and-display" parking meter**, as used in some parts of London and on a trial basis in Boston[45], is a new type of parking meter that allows a single machine to control numerous parking spaces at once. Using these meters would also offer the possibility of instituting higher prices during peak times (or off-peak discounts), providing the ability to fine-tune parking charges in response to time of day, season, and other circumstances. The machines are also easier for the public to use, offering multiple language options and the ability to accept credit and debit cards. Funds raised from the parking program could be used to expand other transportation options or shifted to support other priority areas.

Tour buses present a different set of issues. They are an important form of transportation for school trips, senior citizens, affinity groups and other travelers, and in many ways they represent a vast improvement over visitors arriving by private vehicle. At the same time, tour buses are associated with a range of problems related to loading and unloading, traffic congestion, and idling during layovers. Cities that have responded successfully to these challenges generally have taken steps that include a **well-designed mixture of accommodation and regulation**. In London, for example, on-street bus parking bays are provided in high-demand areas, but buses are charged for the privilege (£4 [$6.75] per hour or more) and are subject to substantial penalties for illegal parking. In Philadelphia, new facilities have made bus loading/unloading and layover parking much more convenient, but the city has stepped up enforcement of no-parking and no-idling regulations in return. Establishing a specific tour bus strategy for Washington involves weighing a number of local factors in conjunction with stakeholders, and is the subject of another study.[46] The lesson from this report is that creative solutions are possible, and that the NPS and its partners should not necessarily shy away from regulatory and pricing strategies, again as long as they are part of a thoughtful and balanced program to manage traffic and improve the visitor experience.

Study the feasibility of a gateway visitor center:

The visitor information center in Savannah is an excellent example of a gateway-type visitor center. At these gateways, car-based visitors can be intercepted prior to reaching the most congested part of the city; they can then park their car, receive orientation information, and transfer to walking, visitor transportation and sightseeing tours, or other forms of ATS. This rolls up many advantages into one building, keeping car traffic out of the dense historic district while also creating a highly visible locus of orientation to enhance the interpretive quality of the visit.

---

[45] http://www.cityofboston.gov/transportation/multispace_meters.asp
[46] Volpe Center tour bus study.

However, Savannah's situation is somewhat unique, and as described above the success of the center depends on a number of attributes coming together in one location. In particular, a gateway center needs a site that is outside of the most congested part of the city, is easily accessible to the main routes, and can accommodate large amounts of car parking, yet is within easy walking (or perhaps shuttle bus) distance of the main visitor attractions. Smaller cities such as Savannah have an easier time aligning all of these factors than large cities like Washington. Philadelphia's Independence Visitor Center is an example of a slightly different approach that might be more suitable to Washington, where the center is sited in the downtown area, close to visitor attractions and public transit, with garage parking available at market rates. Additional research on feasibility and (if appropriate) site selection would help to evaluate the potential for a gateway-type center in Washington.

Specific recommendations for visitor transportation services:

Service characteristics and pricing:

The case studies all show that the traveling public remains interested in narrated, hop-on/hop-off tours of historic downtown areas. This is true even in cities such as Savannah and Philadelphia where free or low-cost shuttle bus service is available along similar routes with similar frequencies. This is an indication that there is a market for both un-narrated and narrated services, and that much of the value of the latter (as revealed in its price premium) lies in the **interpretation** itself. Each city's services are somewhat different, but there was a great deal of consistency about the basic attributes, with the market seeming to have gravitated toward services with **90- to 110-minute loops, with about 15 or 20 stops** that serve top visitor destinations and are well-marked with the company's signage. **Frequencies are usually in the range of every 20 to 30 minutes** during peak times, with an **all-day ticket costing in the range of $20 to $25**. Such strong similarity across cities implies that this service model is one that works well for both the tour operators and the public; it is unlikely to be the only model, however.

Vehicle types:

Choosing specific vehicle types for visitor transportation services involves a number of trade-offs between **fuel type, attractiveness, capacity, maneuverability, and accessibility**. No one vehicle type is optimal in all of these aspects, and the case studies highlight examples of different attempts to balance these factors.

For example, the red double-decker buses used in Philadelphia and London are quite distinctive and are more maneuverable in tight urban spaces than other vehicles of comparable passenger-carrying capacity. They also offer a nice view of the city from the upper level. However, the double-deckers currently used in these cities run on diesel fuel and are not accessible to the handicapped. (Fortunately, newer models of double-decker buses are available that run on alternative fuels and are completely accessible.) The trolley tours of Boston, Savannah, and Philadelphia take another approach, balancing attractiveness with accessibility by using vehicles that resemble antique trolleys but that can also be made accessible. Another approach is that of Orlando's Lynx, which uses low-floor, accessible buses that run on clean-burning natural gas. The modern, utilitarian look of these buses is softened through distinctive public-art exteriors and colorful bus shelters.

Many other types of vehicles are available in numerous permutations, so the NPS has wide latitude in seeking out visitor transportation vehicles that best meet their goals. The case studies all indicate that the public is interested in tour vehicles that are **attractive and unique** (if not downright exotic like the Duck Tours). Less than 5 percent of Americans use public transportation on their daily commute[47], so many visitors may hold a stereotyped view of buses as smelly and unattractive. Tour services in most cities seem to go out of their way to belie this view by using vehicles with aesthetic appeal. The NPS therefore should consider the potential value of attractive or distinctive vehicles, though of course safety and accessibility should not be compromised. Fortunately, we find that **accessibility is not incompatible with attractiveness**, as many of the "vintage" trolleys are accessible and the colorful Lynx Lymmo buses are even more so due to their low-floor design.

Washington is a congested urban area and its region has been designated by the Environmental Protection Agency as a "severe" non-attainment area with respect to ozone emissions[48]. Therefore decisions about vehicle types should also give strong weight to the possibility of using **alternative fuels**, such as the compressed natural gas used by Lynx Lymmo. By doing so, the NPS would have another opportunity to lead by example on issues of environmental sustainability. Another key consideration that emerges from the case studies is that vehicles should be **sensitive to the context** in which they operate. Vintage trolleys are a good fit for historic areas in Boston and Savannah (even though both historic districts pre-date motor vehicles), double-decker buses have long been an icon of London, and exuberantly colored buses seem to capture the spirit of sunny Orlando. Central Washington, with its many important symbols of the nation and memorials for the dead, would seem to call for vehicles that are distinctive, yet dignified rather than vividly colored or dramatically styled.

Types of routes and services:

Findings from the case studies indicate that typical hop-on/hop-off tour loops remain popular. In each city, one of the key elements of these services was locating stops that provide convenient access to the major tourist destinations and are easily recognizable as such. There is also growing interest in **unconventional tours, unique themes and**

---

[47] Census 2000.
[48] http://www.epa.gov/oar/oaqps/greenbk/onc.html

41

approaches, and opportunities for personalization. For example, London's sightseeing tours offer the use of **multiple interconnecting routes** for the cost of a single ticket, giving visitors more choice and customizability. Similarly, a tour provider in Savannah offers, in conjunction with its trolley tours, **longer excursions** that take visitors to interesting neighborhoods and sights that are off of the usual tourist trail.

Alternative and novel **modes of travel** were another recurring theme. Duck Tours, taxicab tours, riverboat tours, walking tours, and bike tours all appeal to segments of the visitor market, particularly to those who are seeking something that is less conventional or "packaged," or to those who want to incorporate some active recreation into their sightseeing. Similarly, a number of tour operators offer special tours of **thematic interest**, such as nighttime ghost tours or tours focusing on architecture. These **walking tours** are popular and can be offered either as separate tours or, as in London, included free with the purchase of an all-day sightseeing ticket.

The implications of these themes for Washington visitor transportation services are diverse, and it bears repeating that it is not necessarily feasible or desirable for the NPS to offer many dozens of tours, employing exotic vehicles and catering to every conceivable interest. However, several potential innovations could at least be considered in light of the case study findings. These would include creating **additional interconnecting visitor transportation and sightseeing loops** reaching out into other areas of Washington; expanding the range of **excursions beyond the National Mall area,** particularly to NPS units that are currently less accessible; and **studying the feasibility of adding a water-based tour option** such as a Potomac River tour. These new services would tap into the strong visitor desires for novel means of transportation, unique experiences, and additional latitude to create customized itineraries. The new services could also increase the desirability of the visitor transportation and sightseeing tours as compared to driving in a number of ways, notably by providing structured tours into less-familiar neighborhoods and offering unique perspectives such as the view of the city from the Potomac. The additional visitor transportation loops could also be a means, as in London, of providing connecting service to hotel districts (more on this below).

Connections to parking, transit, and hotels:

All of the visitor transportation and sightseeing services in our case-study cities recognize the value of being easily accessible to visitors traveling by various modes. Most have tour stops that **connect with local public transit services and downtown parking facilities,** in some cases sharing stops with public transit services. In some cities, tours were also accessible via **park-and-ride services** and stops were located at **regional and inter-city rail stations** to make them accessible to an even wider range of visitors. We did not find any examples of tour operators who provide remote parking facilities and then bus visitors to their trolley route, though some of the Savannah tours have their own welcome centers (with parking) that are outside of the historic district but on the trolley route. In addition, we found examples of tour services that provide **connecting bus transportation to and from suburban and in-town hotels**. The London tours also operate **secondary bus loops** that serve a mixture of hotels and visitor attractions and link up with the main tour routes.

The current NPS visitor transportation services in Washington are already quite convenient to public transit and commercial parking facilities. These connections are worth preserving and enhancing when looking at future visitor transportation services. The stop at Union Station is particularly important since, in addition to its connection to Metrorail, it allows inter-city and suburban railroad passengers to join the tour without any additional travel. As mentioned above, additional transportation links would also be useful at NPS sites, such as the Lincoln and Jefferson memorials and parks outside the downtown area, that are beyond easy walking distance from Metrorail stops. **Connecting bus transportation** from hotels, **additional tour loops** that would serve hotels and historic sites outside of the core, and additional **park-and-ride options** are all enhancements that should be considered as part of an overall strategy for reducing private car travel.

Ticket purchases:

With a few exceptions, most of the tour providers we studied offer multiple ticket-purchase options, so that visitors can buy their tickets ahead of time by telephone or internet or at a street-side kiosk, or simply pay as they board the vehicle. Washington's visitor transportation and sightseeing services already provide these options, and our research did not unearth any new or innovative approaches to ticketing.

Interpretation:

Narrated tours are in strong demand in our case study cities, particularly in those cities with the strongest parallels to Washington. Indeed, narrated tours command a strong price premium over transit buses running along similar routes. The three methods used by the sightseeing services profiled here are: driver-provided narration, live narration by a guide other than the driver, and recorded narration. Each has its own advantages and disadvantages. Live narration creates a more dynamic experience and allows for interaction between passengers and the guide, but limits the potential for multiple languages. Having the driver provide commentary can be a distraction from driving, but is more cost-effective than employing a separate guide. The companies that use separate narrators believe that this creates a small but real marketing advantage over other sightseeing services. All in all, though, the preferred type and extent of narration is a largely matter of individual taste and is most usefully addressed through the NPS' market research in Washington.

The exact nature of the interpretive content is also, to a large extent, a matter for NPS policy determinations about the messages to be conveyed. Given its mission, it is likely that the NPS would be interested in offering interpretation this is less commercial in nature than that offered by the private trolley tours studied here; instead, it would be more focused on the historical and cultural importance of the sites. It would also be worth considering the inclusion of instructional messages about resource protection and the "dos and don'ts" of visitation.

One specific interpretive innovation that is of interest to an important segment of visitors is increased **multilingual options**. These could be provided by providing non-English speakers with handheld devices that provide recorded commentary in the appropriate language, or by using recorded loops rather than live narration on selected vehicles.

Visitor feedback:

Perhaps the most fundamental way of improving visitor transportation services and tailoring them to users' needs is to solicit input from visitors. While those with the strongest opinions – positive and (more often) negative – can always be counted on to write letters and make phone calls, most visitors do not typically make their voices heard. They may even be unaware of whom to contact with a complaint or suggestion. Additional qualitative research, such as **visitor surveys** or even simple suggestion cards, can shed light on how visitors rate their mobility options and overall experience. These efforts can be used to help refine aspects of the visitor transportation services, or, as the Disney example shows, to re-design informational materials to make them more useful and comprehensible.

Large-scale surveys are expensive undertakings and impose something of a burden on respondents, so they should be carried out on a less frequent basis. However, some element of visitor feedback ought to be an **ongoing effort** with many opportunities for visitors to provide input. This allows the services to be adjusted more frequently and also gives a sense of how visitor priorities vary across seasons.

Funding

Our five case study cities offer a number of models for how the capital and operating expenses for visitor-oriented transportation services can be funded, but they are all significantly different from the current visitor transportation services in the National Mall and surrounding park areas and from the NPS's mission. The NPS is not a private company that can rely on paid-in capital, nor is it a special taxing district or a state-funded public transit agency. It does not seek to maximize profit, nor is transportation its raison d'être. As such, it will need to pursue funding strategies that are consistent with its own mission and goals. The case studies demonstrate that in many instances a range of cooperative funding agreements are in place, involving both public sector collaboration and public-private partnerships.

Summary

The NPS is committed to continuing to provide a quality interpretive experience for visitors to the National Mall and surrounding park areas, to reducing the environmental impact of visitation and congestion on resources, and to promoting overall visitor satisfaction. Case-study research from Boston, Savannah, Orlando, Philadelphia, and London has been employed here to suggest a range of strategies that can be adopted to further these goals. Generally, these can be classified as either specific to the visitor transportation services, or as broader strategies for the range of transportation options and information sources available to visitors. Among the former are several potential ways of expanding the range of visitor transportation tour options; enhancing connections to transit stops and hotels; providing multilingual interpretation; and considering vehicles that use alternative fuels, are accessible to the handicapped, and are visually distinctive yet appropriate to their context. Among the latter are efforts to improve public transit information, encourage pedestrian and bicycle travel, make better use of buses, implement demand-management strategies, and study the feasibility of a gateway visitor center. Working together with other interested stakeholders as part of a task force is also presented as a specific strategy, though in fact collaboration with other interested groups and agencies is also a useful complement to almost everything presented here.

APPENDIX

Comparison chart

City	City population	Region population	Annual visitation	Daily transit ridership
Washington, DC	572,000	7,608,000	18,600,000	893,000
Boston	589,000	5,819,000	12,900,000	824,000
Savannah	132,000	293,000	2,200,000	12,333
Orlando	186,000	1,600,000	40,000,000	70,000
Philadelphia	1,517,000	6,188,000	11,200,000	1,000,000
London	7,200,000	14,000,000	28,000,000	7,500,000
Sources:	Census	Census	CVBs	WMATA; MBTA; CAT; Lynx; SEPTA; TfL